Sun Myung Moon & the Unification Church

Sun Myung Moon & the Moon Unification Church

JAMES BJORNSTAD

BETHANY HOUSE PUBLISHERS
MINNEAPOLIS, MINNESOTA 55438
A Division of Bethany Fellowship, Inc.

Formerly published under the title *The Moon Is Not the Son*.

This is a revised edition.

Library of Congress Catalog Card Number 84–70856

ISBN 0–87123–301–0

Copyright © 1976, 1984
James Bjornstad
All Rights Reserved

Published by Bethany House Publishers
A Division of Bethany Fellowship, Inc.
6820 Auto Club Road, Minneapolis, Minnesota 55438

Printed in the United States of America

DEDICATED

to my students at Northeastern
Bible College who never cease
to amaze me by finding some
new religious movement or
practice, and then desiring that
I tell them what it's all about and
how they can reach these people
for Jesus Christ.

JAMES BJORNSTAD is the Academic Dean and Professor of Philosophy and Theology at Northeastern Bible College. He attended City College of New York, received two degrees from Northeastern Bible College (B.R.E., Th.B.), received his Master's Degree in Religious Education from New York Theological Seminary, and has completed his course work for a Ph.D. from New York University.

Among his previously published works are *Twentieth-Century Prophecy, The Transcendental Mirage,* and *Counterfeits at Your Door.*

He is a member of the Evangelical Theological Society and the Evangelical Philosophical Society.

Mr. Bjornstad has done eighteen years of research and study on the religious movements and practices in America. He has also had twelve years of college teaching experience in the area. His lectures on the subject have taken him to universities, conferences and churches throughout America, Canada, and Europe.

Sun Myung Moon and the Unification Church culminates more than eight years of intensive research, dialogue, and continuous interaction with the Unification Church, its leaders, and its theology.

TABLE OF CONTENTS

1. Moon's History Presented...................... 9
2. Moon's Theology Discerned 19
3. Moon's Claims Examined..................... 41
   Notes 53

KEY
to abbreviations of sources used in footnotes

DP = *Divine Principle* (Washington, D.C.: The Holy Spirit Association for the Unification of World Christianity, 1973)

DPA = Young Oon Kim, *The Divine Principle and Its Application* (Belvedere Tarrytown, New York: The Holy Spirit Association for the Unification of World Christianity, n.d.)

DPSG = *The Divine Principle Study Guide* (Belvedere Tarrytown, New York: The Holy Spirit Association for the Unification of World Christianity, May 1, 1973)

PC = Young Whi Kim, *The Principle of Creation* (Belvedere Tarrytown, New York: The Holy Spirit Association for the Unification of World Christianity, March 15, 1973)

UT = *Unification Thought* (New York, New York: Unification Thought Institute, 1973)

UTCT = Young Oon Kim, *Unification Theology & Christian Thought* (New York: Golden Gate Publishing Co., 1975)

UTSG = *Unification Thought Study Guide* (New York, New York: Unification Thought Institute, January 30, 1974)

1

MOON'S HISTORY PRESENTED

Young Myung Moon was born in a Presbyterian family on January 6, 1920, in the Pyungan Buk-do province of what is now North Korea. (His name was later changed to Sun Myung Moon.)

From his earliest childhood he has always been interested in spiritism, but it was not until he was 16 years old that his first important encounter occurred. That was on an Easter Sunday morning in 1936 when "Jesus" appeared to him while he was in prayer and "revealed that he was destined to accomplish a great mission in which Jesus would work with him."[1] Some say that he was actually told to restore God's perfect kingdom, while others say he was told by Jesus that he would be "the completer of man's salvation by being the Second Coming of Christ."

Experiences like this and other spiritualistic phenomena play a large part in Rev. Moon's life and theology. Rev. Moon continually receives "new revelations," practices a form of soul travel whereby he allegedly projects himself into the spirit realm to see Jesus and the saints, and claims to be an "expert" on the spirit world.

In the nine years following this initial experience of importance, the contents of the *Divine Principle* were developed, according to his followers. During this time he was a student in the field of electrical engineering in Japan, and also a self-taught Bible student. The latter, of course, provided the basis for his reworking of the Bible.

After World War II, while living in North Korea, he became involved with a group that was deeply entrenched in mystical revelations, awaiting the impending appearance of a new Messiah. They also believed that Korea was the New Jerusalem of the Bible and that the Messiah would be born in Korea. These elements are all found in Rev. Moon's theology and in the *Divine Principle*.

In 1945, Rev. Moon had his most important experience. He tells us of this in *Master Speaks*, but perhaps the most succinct statement of it is found in the claims of the Unification Church itself:

> At that moment, he became the absolute victor of heaven and earth. The whole spirit world bowed down to him on that day of victory. . . . The spirit world has already recognized him as the victor of the universe and the Lord of creation.[2]

The *Divine Principle* mentions this experience by saying that "he fought alone against myriads of satanic forces, both in the spirit and physical world, and finally triumphed over them all."[3]

Shortly thereafter, he changed his birth name to Sun Myung Moon which means "Shining Sun and Moon"—a title savoring of divinity and of the whole universe.

Following this, while still residing in North Korea, Rev. Moon was sent to jail. His followers say that it was because of his anti-communism, while others say it was for bigamy and adultery. A former North Korean army officer who was in prison with Rev. Moon says that Moon received a seven-year sentence for contributing to "social disorder," proclaiming the imminent coming of the second messiah in Korea.[4]

He was released from jail in 1950 when the United Nations forces under General Douglas MacArthur entered North Korea. He moved down to Pusan in South Korea, where he became a harbor laborer. In 1954, he founded his church in Seoul: it was officially called the Holy Spirit Association for the Unification of World Christianity. In the same year his first wife left him. "She did not understand my religion," Rev. Moon explains.

In 1955, he was arrested and placed in jail again, this time in South Korea. The government charged him with draft evasion and later with adultery and promiscuity. His followers explain how the moral charges occurred by stating that in the early years of the church, meetings were held in the homes of his followers, most of whom were women. Because the meetings would go until the early hours of the morning, rumors began to develop and spread that these were affairs.

On the other side, Rev. Won Il Chei, a leading Presbyterian minister in Seoul, says, "If we believe those who have gone into this group and come out, they say that one has to receive Sun Myung Moon's blood to receive salvation. That blood is ordinarily received by three periods of sexual intercourse."[5]

Whatever the reason, the government failed to prove its case against Rev. Moon. Thus the Unification Church can say, as W. Farley Jones, director of its Public Information Office, did in his letter to the *Christian Century* magazine, that the morals charges were dropped and that the "Korean Court records document this."[6]

The year 1957 brought about the publication of the *Divine Principle*, a volume written not by Rev. Moon, as many people think, but by one of his followers, Yee Hye Wen. This is the Unification Church's interpretation of the Bible. This volume sets forth Moon's teachings and, as the *Divine Principle* itself states, it is only "part of the truth."[7]

Some within the church have indicated that there are areas which need refining and reworking in the *Divine Principle*, such as the statement that there are many direct parallels between the "Babylonian Captivities" (i.e., a comparison of Israel and Judah's fate under the Babylonians, with the Papal problems of the Roman Catholic Church in the fourteenth and fifteenth centuries).[8] Some believe that a whole new volume is needed.

It is interesting to note that regarding the English translations alone, the second edition (1973) is different from the first edition (1966) in quite a few areas. Any comparison of these two editions would easily reveal this.

Soon thereafter, Rev. Moon developed his business enterprises, which included gingseng tea, titanium products, pharmaceuticals and air rifles. He became a wealthy man, and, as his wealth increased, so did his standing in the community. Finally in the mid 1960s he launched a vigorous campaign against communism which brought him the support of South Korea's leader, Park Chung Hee.

January 1, 1972, was a major turning point in the ministry of his church. "God" appeared to him and told him to come to America. A 22-acre estate in Tarrytown, New York, was purchased as the American headquarters, providing an elaborate training center for his followers as well as a mansion for his family.

In 1974, after some crusades and rallies, he began to speak out stronger on behalf of America, and especially on behalf of the President, Richard Nixon. In fact, he led a pro-Nixon rally on the steps of the Nation's capitol. In other cities his followers also held similar rallies. But it was not long afterward that Nixon resigned.

From America an international emphasis was initiated in 1975. Rev. Moon assigned three missionaries to each of ninety-five new countries. Furthermore, crusade teams would be sent out on three-month tours beginning with four selected countries.[9]

> In recent years, Moon has attempted to set up a financial base in Uruguay but was forced to stop trying to win converts in that country owing to strong Roman Catholic opposition. Although conversions are few, financial investments by the church have been substantial and tax breaks from Uruguayan government leader Gen. Gregorio Alvarez have helped the Unification Church.[10]

In its brief history, the Unification Church has encountered many rejections in its quest for approval by religious councils and groups. These groups include the Presbyterian Church in Korea, a Korean Council of Churches and several council of churches here in America, including some for whom this rejection was their very first refusal of anyone. There are also some denominations which have spoken out against the Unification Church by way of resolutions or other statements. As far as we can tell, none accepted them.

In spite of this the Unification Church continues to attract many young people. It seems that these young people find therein an alternative lifestyle that does not demand sexual performance, radical politics or drug participation; yet it allows them to live in a commune, work hard and hope to improve the lot of fellowman. Some are inspired by messianic hopes that their children will not have to grow up and live in a world like this one, but as perfected children under the Lord of the Second Advent.

Controversy reigns over these converts to Rev. Moon. Many families throughout the United States have contacted the state and local authorities regarding their children who have gone into the Unification Church, complaining of some type of mind control or mind influence over their child. Many ex-members of the church have testified that this was the case with them.

One of the most interesting examples involved a newspaper reporter working under cover. He went to one of the centers and participated. During his stay there he found himself overwhelmed and began confessing to one of the other initiates that he was a reporter. His remarks were interesting and bear out the effectiveness of their training program: "How could it happen, I thought. I had been there two and a half days. I found Moon's principles unbelievable. Yet I suddenly fell off guard."[11]

To understand the process of what actually happens at these centers, one should read the article on "Brainwashing" in the *Encyclopaedia Britannica*. Though not written on the Unification Church, one can easily note the various stages involved in breaking down the ego structure. With any knowledge of the actions and activities in a center, the article relates to and identifies that which is used by the Unification Church.

Years ago involuntary conversion was achieved through physical coercion. Torture of this nature is still in force today, as a recent *Time* magazine article brought out.[12] But in the past few decades a different method is being used to bring about conversion. It is a psychosocial form of coercion. This is the means used in Unification centers. The first step is isolation, where one is removed from the usual cultural support system of his or her pattern of behavior. To prevent one from leaving the new environment, they use psychology: "How can you forsake us and leave? We love you so very much." (This is called "love bombing.") Or, "Satan is trying to pull you away from God because you have been called and chosen to build the Kingdom of heaven. Don't give in to Satan."

The second step is willingness, which is usually already accomplished because the person freely comes to the center. From here on it is only a matter of modifying the thoughts and behavior in a controlled social environment. The initiate is expected to conform to the group's perception of reality—i.e., his actions and thoughts become that of the group. So completely is this accomplished that the following account by an ex-Moonie only begins to reveal the great transformation: "Adjusting to the outside world again was like arriving on another planet. Driving my car, balancing my checkbook, watching TV and reading books besides Moon's *Divine Principle* were strange. It took a long time to fill the vacuum that had been created inside me."[13]

One of the representatives of the Unification Church explained the above procedure by saying, "It is not brainwashing. It's purely a system of indoctrination, the same as you Christians use." Let it be clearly understood that what the Unification Church does is more than indoctrination because of the controlled environment it uses, and more than Christian conversion because it does not rely solely on personal decisions and personal choices.

This is not to say that every person involved in the

Unification Church is "brainwashed." Some accept the theology because they agree with it. Nonetheless, the procedure is used in conjunction with the teaching to reinforce it and bring about one's accepting it.

Deprogramming, on the other hand, is merely the above procedure in reverse.[14] The method is the same with the exception of those abducted in some manner (their willingness develops in the controlled environment). The content used is totally different. Instead of continually hearing good things about Rev. Moon, they now continually hear bad things. As one deprogrammer expressed it, "It's fighting fire with fire."

One word of distinction should be noted here. Deprogramming is not Christian conversion. In the former the old pattern or program is broken, creating a religious vacuum in that life which if not filled can cause those who have been deprogrammed to return to the former religious movement. The Bible describes this procedure and its problem in Matthew 12:43-45:

> Now when the unclean spirit goes out of a man, it passes through waterless places, seeking rest, and does not find it. Then it says, I will return to my house from which I came; and when it comes, it finds it unoccupied, swept, and put in order. Then it goes, and takes along with it seven other spirits more wicked than itself, and they go in and live there; and the last state of that man becomes worse than the first.

The latter, Christianity, differs in that the Holy Spirit comes into that person's being and begins the process of recreation. This happens when that person accepts Jesus as Lord and Savior.

To summarize, the history of the Unification Church, as well as that of Rev. Moon, is marked with controversy. But, in the midst of that history, a strange theology was formulated which provides the foundation for the Unification Church. It is that theology which we need to examine next. It provides not only the basis for their beliefs but for all their practices as well. Throughout this section, glimpses of this theology have been revealed in the various experiences, encounters, and problems. Once you note the theology, then some of the aspects of this history will take on even more significance. Then, you will also know what it is they are trying to get you to believe and become involved in.

2

MOON'S THEOLOGY DISCERNED

If you have ever spoken to a member of the Unification Church, you have undoubtedly noticed how "Christian" their statements appeared to be. Did you notice the abundance of biblical terms and phrases used, such as born again, salvation, sin, only one God, one Christ, one Bible, Satan is the ruler of this world, and the day of the Second Coming of Christ?

In the midst of all this "Christian" terminology, many have become confused and some even fooled as to exactly what Rev. Moon and the Unification Church believe and teach. There is a reason for this confusion. It stems from the fact that they use biblical phrases and words; but they have rejected biblical definitions and substituted Moon's definitions.

Let me illustrate this problem for you. One day, I noticed a small gathering of people. They were grouped around a young lady who, with the aid of a blackboard, was lecturing them on how science supported theology. She was a member of the Unification Church. I stood in the back of the group and listened. Finally an elderly lady, who had been there longer than I, turned and said to me, "They sound Christian to me. After all, they do talk about God and Jesus, and seem to have a real zeal and love for the Lord." And with that she left, absolutely convinced that what that follower of Rev. Moon was saying was biblical.

There is a lesson to be learned from this episode. It has to do with the process she used to arrive at her conclusion. You see, she listened to the message and she heard familiar terms, Christian terms, but she made one great mistake. She interpreted those terms with her definition, and since she did not know the Unification definition, she thought the young lady was a Christian. She made no attempt to discern what that follower of Rev. Moon meant by those terms, and thus saw no difference. I'm sure if that member of the Unification Church had been pressed theologically, that woman would have seen a difference.

We must not make the same error. The definition of a word depends on the content one gives to it and/or the context in which one uses it. Therefore in order to know and understand what a person means when using a word, as in the case of this follower of Rev. Moon, we must understand what they mean by it first, and then compare that to what we mean by those terms. Only then can we discover whether they are really the same.

This language problem is precisely what Paul had in mind in 2 Corinthians 11:13–15, in which he vividly presents the fact that there are those who present "another Jesus," who represent "another gospel," and who impart "another spirit." For our purposes, we will only consider Paul's warning regarding "another Jesus." (The same could be demonstrated regarding "another spirit" and "another gospel.")

Virtually every religious movement in America today mentions Jesus Christ. In fact, He is an integral part of their theologies. They all use the same word Jesus, but their definitions contradict one another.

Consider some of these religious movements, noting carefully that each one presents Jesus, but with a different meaning. The Jesus of Christian Science is a divine ideal or principle, inherent within every man, and Jesus is its supreme manifestation; while the Jesus of the Jehovah's Witnesses is Michael the Archangel, prior to his divesting himself of his angelic nature and appearing in the world as a perfect man, as "a god." The Jesus of Mormonism is one god among many, while the Jesus of Spiritism is a pantheistic manifestation of Deity. The Jesus of Bahai is one of nine human messengers, while the Jesus of Meher Baba is one of many personifications or incarnations of God. The Jesus of Hinduism is one of many great teachers or gurus, an Avantaric form of Deity, while the Jesus of Christianity is the unique incarnation of God, "God manifested in the flesh." Each of the above religions use the same word Jesus. They all speak and teach about Jesus. Yet every one of them presented a different doctrine as to who He is. They all use the same word and they all mean something completely different by it.

Therefore it is absolutely necessary that we understand what people mean when using theological words. Dr. Young Oon Kim, professor of systematic theology and world religions at Unification Theological Seminary, makes this very point in the beginning of her book *Unification Theology & Christian Thought*. She says that in order to understand or even attempt to understand theology, one must first begin by understanding what is meant by the word "God."[1] In fact, all Unification literature regarding theology begins with the attempt to understand God through the creation, and then continues to build its theology on that doctrine.[2] The importance of starting with an understanding of the word God is best stated by Dr. Emil Brunner, whom Dr.

Kim quotes and is in agreement with on this point. "Indeed if one rightly understands that which the Bible means by the Creator, he has rightly understood the whole Bible. Everything else is involved in this one word."[3] But, just as there are many concepts of Jesus, as noted above, so also there are many diverse concepts concerning God. Thus it is imperative to understand what Rev. Moon means by the word God. After all, it is the initial difference between a right and a wrong understanding of theology. When he speaks of God, who or what is his God? Likewise, when he uses the name Jesus, who is his Jesus?

In order to discover this and to know and understand his theology (that which is presented in *Divine Principle* and taught by the Unification Church), we must take care to interpret his words and phrases in his theological context, using only the content which he gives to them. This is not the easiest task because his theology is eclectic in nature, and occasionally contains his own unique terminology which one must understand in order to perceive his theology.

The following is Rev. Moon's basic theology in simplified fashion. It is not meant to be comprehensive or overly detailed, but merely a broad general outline constructed from the various writings of the Unification Church according to selected categories. To help understand clearly what he is saying, and at the same time to distinguish it from what he is not saying, his theology has been placed in contradistinction to the theology of the Bible.

I. Who or What Is God?

Rev. Moon—Spirit/Energy

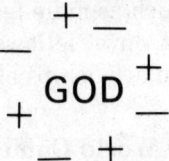

Ultimately God is an invisible essence manifesting dual qualities—spirit and energy from which all existence generates.[4] Thus, with regard to the creation, God is set forth as "perpetual, self-generating energy."[5] As Dr. Kim states, "The energy, the force behind all matter, is God's external form. . . ."[6] God also manifests dual polarity through paired relationships, such as male and female, positive and negative[7]—similar in essence to the yin (male) and yang (female) principles of Taoist philosophy.[8]

Yet in this manifestation, God is also set forth as a personal God,[9] having consciousness, intelligence, love and purpose.[10]

Christianity—Spirit

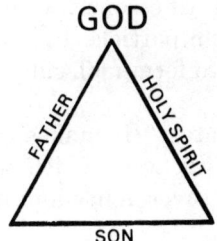

"God is Spirit" (John 4:24). He is personal, infinite, eternal and complete in himself. God is One, yet eternally exists as three persons: Father, Son and Holy Spirit (not dual polarity such as male-female, etc.); one unity (Tri-unity) in which love, fellowship, communication and interpersonal relationships always exist.

II. How Did the World Come Into Existence?

Rev. Moon—Projected Out of God

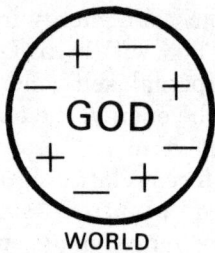

Creation, including the world, is the outward form of the invisible essence called God.[11] The whole creation "is his body or outward form."[12] Thus God's creation activity is the emanation or projection, both physically and spiritually, of His essence. "God projected His heart and energy to form particles . . . particles . . . to form atoms . . . atoms to form molecules, molecules to form minerals. . . ."[13]

As Dr. Kim states: "He makes His presence known in the totality of creation which serves as His body, exemplifying His sovereignty and providing the outer form of His being."[14]

Note: Rev. Moon's theology is *Monistic*. It sets forth

the explanation and existence of everything ultimately in one essence or substance which is God.

Christianity—Created Out of Nothing

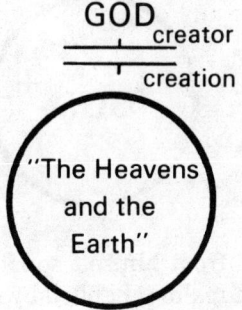

God created the world out of nothing. The creation is not God nor His outward form. It is separate and distinct from His being. It did not emanate nor project from His essence (Gen. 1, 2; Ps. 33:6; Heb.11:3; etc.).

The creation declares the handiwork of God (Ps. 19:1) and one should realize from observing the creation that a personal God made it (Rom. 1:20), not that it is God or an extension of His being.

Note: Christian theology is *Theistic*. It sets forth the existence of a personal creator God as distinct in essence from the creation He made.

III. How Did Man Come Into Existence?

Rev. Moon—Projection of God

God projected from himself spirit beings in a sub-level existence, "a realm inhabited by spirits which have not yet grown to even the form level."[15] A spirit becomes a form spirit when it is born into a body in this world where it can develop a personality.[16] Each person has a spirit man and a physical man.[17]

Initially two of these, Adam and Eve, began in the garden of Eden.[18] They, like men and women after them, are the "external and objective manifestation of the polarity of God,"[19] an extension of God out in the physical world.[20] Each person is "one unique part of God's Infinite Nature."[21]

Christianity—Created by God

Men and women are created in the image of God, but not as a part of God. Man is the creature; God, the Creator. This distinction is never blurred in the Bible. God, being external to creation and distinct from it, took the dust of the ground, breathed into it giving it life, and man was created (Gen. 2:7). Together with Eve, whom God fashioned from a part of man, Adam was placed in the garden of Eden. It was there that God met with them and their fellowship was personal (Gen. 1-3).

IV. How Did Man Break His Relationship With God?

Rev. Moon—Fornication With Lucifer

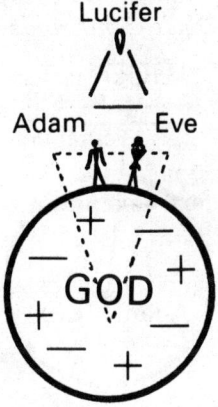

Adam and Eve were placed in the garden of Eden to develop themselves through the stages of "formation," "growth" and "perfection."[22] The ideal goal was marriage once maturity (i.e. perfection) was attained.[23] It was at this point that "Adam and Eve would have formed a trinity with God"[24] and would have been able to "produce children free of inherited sin."[25] However, before they could attain perfection, Eve committed fornication with Lucifer. Lucifer and Eve became one in sexual union, causing the spiritual fall of mankind.[26] Eve, hoping to undo her action, persuaded Adam to live with her as husband, even though he had not attained perfection either. This caused the physical fall of mankind.[27]

Through sexual union, Eve took on the sinful characteristics of Lucifer, and Adam received these sinful characteristics through his sexual union with Eve.[28] Thus the entire course of human history deviated from the "divine principle" of maturing to perfection first, then marrying and producing perfect children.[29]

Christianity—Disobedience to God's Commands

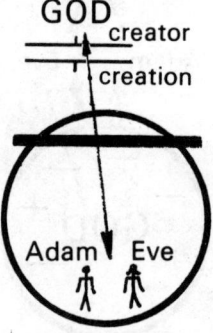

Adam and Eve were placed in the garden of Eden to care for it and to live there in perfect fellowship with God. They were told to be fruitful, multiply and fill up the earth (Gen. 1:28ff.). They were also told not to eat of one tree in the garden. However, Adam and Eve chose to disobey God. Their sin, according to God, was: "Have you eaten of the tree of which I commanded you not to eat of?" (not "Did you commit fornication with Lucifer?" See Genesis 3:11). Eve responded by saying, "The serpent deceived me and I ate" (not "The serpent deceived me and I committed fornication." See Genesis 3:14). This initial act of disobedience in eating of that which God had forbidden has affected the entire course of human history (Gen. 3:14–19; Rom. 5:15, 17; etc.). Man's basic problem is that he has sinned before a holy and righteous God, thus alienating himself from his Creator in his heart and mind. Even today man continues to rebel against God and disobey Him as did his original parents, Adam and Eve.

V. How Can Man Become Right With God?

Rev. Moon—Jesus Failed in His Mission

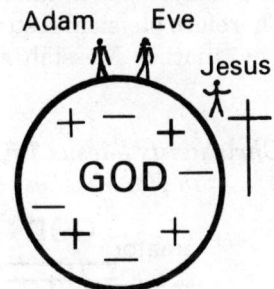

Salvation is basically the undoing of the results of the Fall. The individual has to be restored and perfected, and then enter into a marriage relationship and produce perfect children.[30] To accomplish this, a Messiah or a Christ is needed.[31]

Historically, Jesus the Messiah came in Adam's place

to restore mankind. He was not Deity; ". . . it is a great error to think Jesus was God Himself."[32] Jesus on earth "was a man no different from us except for the fact that He was without original sin."[33]

Jesus' purpose in coming was to take a bride in Eve's place, marry and produce perfect children.[34] By the example and power of his family, other perfect families would be formed until the whole of society was restored and in line with God's purpose.[35]

Jesus *failed* in His mission. He was crucified before He could marry.[36] It was never God's predetermined purpose that He die.[37] It was the failure of John the Baptist that was "the major cause of the crucifixion of Jesus."[38] Because of this, God allowed Jesus to die. "Satan invaded the physical body of Jesus and crucified him."[39]

Jesus was resurrected from the dead as a spirit man, thus redeeming man spiritually.[40] At this point God could claim the souls of men, but could not give redemption to the body.[41] Jesus failed to redeem man physically.[42] Therefore physical restoration is still to be accomplished by another Messiah at the Second Advent.[43]

Christianity—Jesus Triumphed in His Mission

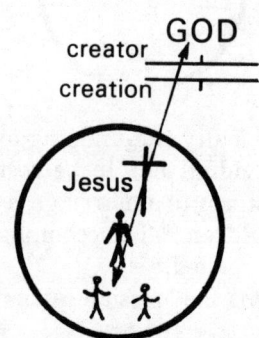

Salvation is exclusively God's provision for our sins through the death of His Son on Calvary's cross. Man cannot attain it, work for it or buy it. It is a free gift. One must recognize his condition before God as a sinner, confess his sins to God, believe that Jesus died in his place on the cross as payment for his sins (Jesus himself being without sin), and trust in Jesus Christ alone for a right relationship with God (Gal. 2:16; Eph. 2:8, 9).

Historically, God took the initiative in the incarnation or Christ's first coming to redeem mankind. Jesus was fully God and fully man (Isa. 7:14; 9:6; John 1:1; 5:18; 10:30; etc.). Jesus' death was to pay the price for our sins. The Old Testament sacrificial system, along with numerous passages in both the Old and New Testaments, states that the Messiah had to die (Isa. 53; Ps. 27:13–18; Heb. 9:1ff.; 10:1ff.; etc.). Marriage was not the goal and His death was not a mistake (Acts 2:23). It was predetermined that God would provide salvation in this way and offer it as a free gift to all who would accept His Son Jesus as Lord and Savior (Rom. 5:8–11; Gal. 1:14).

His bodily resurrection from the dead guarantees that He has redeemed man totally (physically and spiritually), and His return to this earth one day will bring about this completion in the lives of His children (Rom. 8:23, 24; 1 John 3:2, 3; 1 Cor. 15:1ff.; etc.).

Rev. Moon—Another Messiah

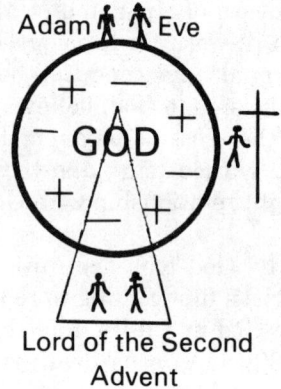

Lord of the Second Advent

"The Lord of the Second Advent is to be born on the earth as the King of Kings."[44] We are not to expect the return of Jesus himself,[45] but another Messiah—a man who will be born in Korea.[46] (Rev. Moon was born in Korea.) He will be confirmed as the Messiah through the spirit world.[47] (Rev. Moon was confirmed in this manner.)

Though one may have his spirit man perfected by believing in Jesus, it will not help his physical man. Thus the Lord of the Second Advent will provide additional revelation[48] (Rev. Moon has a new revelation) which will enable the physical man to be perfected, thus completing the work of salvation.

A new age dawned in 1960: "At that time, the marriage of the lamb prophesied in the 19th chapter of Revelation took place. Thus, the Lord of the Second Advent and His Bride became the True Parents of mankind...."[49] (1960 happens to be the year in which Rev. Moon married his present wife Hak-Ja Han.) This Messiah will establish the perfect family, the task that Jesus never fulfilled.[50] Other perfect families will be formed, which will produce a perfect society that will spread to the entire world.[51]

In the 1980s the new Messiah will be revealed to the world (it appears that Rev. Moon is that person). When he declares the Kingdom, the life spirits of those who have lived before will join the followers of Rev. Moon so that they can develop into divine spirits.[52] Evil people will go through a similar reincarnation procedure.[53] The law of Karma is operative in this procedure, for "if any arrive in the spirit world with unpaid debts, they will have to work to assist perhaps the very ones they hurt in order to pay what they owe."[54]

All the religions of the world will be unified,[55] which will bring about unification among all peoples.[56] Everyone will eventually be saved and perfected. The earth will be restored through the efforts of science.[57]

Christianity—Jesus Returns

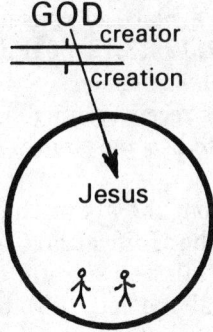

Because Jesus rose bodily from the dead, He lives today and is returning to this earth one day from heaven (not born as a man) to consummate His plan for the ages (Acts 1:11; 1 Thess. 4:13–17; Rev. 20:1ff.). Redemption, both spiritual and physical, is complete in Him. We receive this completion at the resurrection when Jesus returns (1 Cor. 15:20ff.), when we shall be like Him in the sense that we shall have a soul and body incapable of sin: not earthly, but heavenly. We shall reign with Jesus in His kingdom for a thousand years here on earth. The present heavens and earth will be purged and redeemed. New heavens and a new earth will be brought forth, where those who love Jesus shall live forever in His presence and fellowship.

There is no "Third Adam" or "New Messiah" needed, for what was effected by the disobedience of the first Adam in the garden of Eden was remedied by the Second Adam, Jesus Christ. Everyone who accepts Jesus as his personal Savior and Lord has right standing before God, and is assured of an eternal relationship with Him. Those who reject Him, at death are placed into Hades. At the second resurrection these will be cast into the Lake of Fire. At death this means eternal separation from God in a place of conscious torment (Rev. 20:13ff.; Matt. 8:11, 12; 13:42–50; Luke 16:19–31; 2 Pet. 2:17; Jude 13; etc.).

"But as many as received him [Jesus Christ], to them gave he the right to become the children of God" (John 1:12).

It is obvious from the above that Rev. Moon's theology and that of the Unification Church has a unique definitive content all its own, and that it is quite different from biblical theology. From the initial differences of the Creator and the creation right down to the end-time product, they are two separate and distinct theologies.

Interestingly, though, members of the Unification Church generally attempt to stay away from these differences, at least initially in their contacts with outsiders. While speaking one night in a church in New Hampshire, a pioneer of the Unification Church was in the audience. After the meeting was over, he told me who he was and informed me that he had come into that town to develop a Unification center. I asked him why he had accepted Rev. Moon's theology as true. He told me, "Because it clarifies everything in the *Bible*; it's the fulfillment of what the *Bible* teaches."

I asked him to consider a few areas of theology, comparing what the *Bible* stated and what the *Divine Principle* stated, and then to tell me honestly how the *Divine Principle* clarified or fulfilled the teachings of the *Bible*. The *Bible* states: "For in him [Jesus] all the fulness of Deity dwells in bodily form,"[58] while the *Divine Principle* states that Jesus "can by no means be God Himself."[59] The *Bible* states that Jesus was "delivered up by the predetermined plan and foreknowledge of God,"[60] while the *Divine Principle* states that it was not God's plan for Jesus to die.[61] The *Bible* states that Jesus rose bodily from the dead: Jesus said, "A spirit does not have flesh and bones as you see that I have,"[62] while the *Divine Principle* states that Jesus did not rise bodily from the dead, but as a spirit man.[63] The *Bible* states that "this Jesus, who has been taken up from you into heaven, will come in just the same way as you have watched him go into heaven,"[64] while the *Divine Principle* states that Jesus will not return physically to this earth to set up His kingdom.[65] "How would you explain these statements?" I asked him. His reply was, "I'm really sorry. I don't know very much about the Bible." (Sometimes this is just a polite way of saying, "I'm not really interested in what you're saying.") And still he believed that the *Divine Principle* was a clarification or fulfillment of the teachings of the Bible.

Upon what basis could such an understanding be

held? Certainly anyone can see that the *Divine Principle* neither clarifies nor fulfills what the *Bible* teaches. *It denies what the Bible states.* In fact, the *Divine Principle* is a rejection of all previous theological systems and world religions.

On another occasion a member of the Unification Church considered the differences between the *Divine Principle* and the *Bible* and merely dismissed it by saying, "You're a Fundamentalist. You take the Bible too lilterally." (This answer has been ingrained in them from the *Divine Principle*, which states that Christians today "are captive to scriptural words . . . according to the limits of what the New Testament words literally state."[66]) I replied, "That's quite a charge; but is what you claim really so?" "When you read a piece of literature," I continued, "what procedure do you use to understand it?" I said to him, "Look at it this way. When any person writes something, he or she writes it with only one meaning in mind. True?" He thought for a moment and then said, "Yes." "Then the interpretation of any document or piece of literature, be it a fragment of some pre-Socratic philosopher or a page from some medieval mystic, has as its goal the recovery of the exact meaning of the author. Right?" He replied, "Right." "And in order to discover that meaning we must use proper literary, historical and grammatical principles."[67] He agreed.

I opened up my Bible and said, "Consider Luke 24, verse 39. First of all, Luke's purpose in writing is historical—a factual account of what occurred (Luke 1:1–4). He lived at that time, knew the people involved and had access to all of the facts and could check them out. He was a physician, and thus a man of learning. Secondly, the occasion of this verse is after the death of Jesus; the context, the fright of the disciples who, having seen Jesus, thought He was a spirit. Jesus' reply to that was that 'a spirit does not have flesh and bones as you see that I have.' In fact, as you read further on, He even ate broiled fish which substantiates what He said about His bodily resurrection. Thirdly, we also have other historical evidence which corroborates the factuality of Luke's account, the statement of Jesus, and the fact that He rose bodily from the dead."

I asked him if he saw any evidence or anything that would provide a different interpretation. He said, "No." I asked him, "Is that what Luke had in mind when he wrote his gospel, that Jesus rose bodily from the dead?" Finally he admitted it was so, and then concluded with the statement, "But the Bible is wrong there." The final position we came to is that a proper interpretation of the *Bible* and the *Divine Principle* will only yield the conclusion that these are two separate and distinct theologies and that both cannot be right. The discussion now settled on which was true.

The response of the members of the Unification Church in the above encounters can easily be understood when one realizes that they have been taught those statements in their training and believe them because the Unification Church taught it. Rev. Moon himself instructs his church leaders: "Until our mission with the Christian church is over, we must quote the Bible and use it to explain the Divine Principle. After we receive the inheritance of the Christian church we will be free to teach without the Bible."[68] Since I'm a fisherman at heart, it appears from the above that the Unification Church uses the Bible as bait to draw one into its Unification theology, which is totally different from the Bible. Once the bait is uncovered, then you see the hook—a different theology all together.

On still other occasions, members of the Unification

Church have used the theme of unification in their approach. "Wouldn't it be nice if we could all get together; if the world was one big happy family?" Of course this is purported to be the mission of the new Messiah, the Lord of the Second Advent.[69]

Is Rev. Moon's theology really that in which all of Christianity as well as all of the world's religions can find fulfillment? As you compared his theology with that of Christian theology earlier in this chapter, did you see any areas of agreement? Is there any theology which could provide a common basis for all religions?

Certainly it is true that religions have something in common, or else the generic term would not exist. However, the closer one approaches an unarguable common denominator, the closer one comes to pure formality. (Try this with the dog category and see if you can come up with one dog which would be expressive of all the others.) The only theology that could provide a broad enough basis to include all other religions and thus unify them would be a theology that said nothing. A theology which unites all of the religions of the world is simply nonexistent.

Furthermore, the theology of Rev. Moon and that of Christianity, when compared to each other, leaves us with two complete and diverse systems in and of themselves. *They cannot both be true.* The logical impossibility of this rests upon the de facto character of these two theologies themselves. To illustrate: Jesus said, "I am the way, the truth and the life: no man comes to the Father, but by me."[70] Peter states of Jesus: "Neither is there salvation in any other: for there is no other name under heaven given among men, whereby we must be saved."[71] Since Christianity and the *Bible* teach that Jesus Christ is the sole source of human salvation, and Rev. Moon and the *Divine Principle* teach that a future

Messiah is to be the sole source of salvation, they cannot both be true. One denies the other. That is why Rev. Moon and the Unification Church teach that Jesus failed in His mission.

Unification theology is not the unifier of all of the world's religions nor of Christianity. It is the rejection of all of them. It presents the option of choosing Rev. Moon and rejecting all others. In private meetings Rev. Moon has stated, "God is now throwing Christianity away and is establishing a new religion."[72] Many times Rev. Moon has told his listeners—Protestants, Roman Catholics and Jews—that "they will have to make a choice" between their original faiths and his church.[73] One of Rev. Moon's spokesmen, "God's Colonel" Bo Hi Pak, while lecturing in Boston, spoke out against Billy Graham ("He can't tell you how the Messiah is coming."), Christian churches ("They keep watching for big signals from the blue sky."), and others.[74] These were all presented as though they were foolish attempts, and then the theology of Rev. Moon was set forth as truth.

Unquestionably, Rev. Moon's theology is separate and distinct from Christian theology—they are mutually exclusive. You are left with the ultimate decision. Jesus would have you choose Him and reject Rev. Moon. Rev. Moon would have you reject Christianity and accept him.

To determine which theology is worthy of our credence and allegiance requires serious attention to Pilate's question "What is truth?"[75] Which of these theologies is true? Which presents the true doctrine of God and of Jesus Christ? With this in mind, we need to examine the claims of Rev. Moon and his theology in the light of the evidence to see whether it is truth.

One Unification member said to me, "We both love Jesus, and that's the important thing." I pointed out that the Jesus of the Unification Church whom she believed in was different from the Jesus of the Bible whom I believed in. The object of our faith, belief and devotion was different. Her look exhibited the common response, "Why all this semantic nonsense? What does it really matter?" She replied, "You're familiar with the Bible. Jesus said, 'By their fruits you shall know them.' "[76] And with that she told me how much good the Unification Church was doing, how they were (at that time) cleaning up the streets in Manhattan, and the like. I pointed out that she should read the next few verses of that passage in Matthew 7 to note the all-important issue: "Not every one who says to me, Lord, Lord, will enter the kingdom of heaven. . . . Many will say to me in that day, 'Lord, Lord, Look at all the good works we did in your name [my paraphrase]."[77] "Notice Jesus' response," I said, "to these 'good people.' 'I never knew you. Depart from me, you who practice lawlessness.' "[78] "You see," I continued, "the most important issue is a correct understanding of Jesus Christ and a personal relationship with Him as your Lord and Savior. All of the fruits or good works mean nothing if you miss this point."

3

MOON'S CLAIMS EXAMINED

"With the fulness of time, God has sent His messenger to resolve the fundamental questions of life and the universe. His name is Sun Myung Moon."[1]

These words from the *Divine Principle* express the great expectations of the Unification Church and the claims of its founder, Rev. Moon. But how do we know they are true? How do we know that Rev. Moon is not a man deluded by visions of power and grandeur, or a fraud living luxuriously off the unsuspecting, or one deceived by a very clever evil supernatural power—Satan himself? Surely these are viable alternatives. How do we know which of these is true?

Questions like these were asked of several members of the Unification Church. Once the initial reaction was overcome, the general responses were reiterations of Rev. Moon being a messenger of God. As one young lady stated it: "I *know* beyond a shadow of a doubt that Rev. Moon is God's messenger and that his revelations are true." This answer would be fine if the question was "Do you believe Rev. Moon is a messenger of God?" But it certainly does not answer *how* you know this is so. If you repeat the question or rephrase it, stressing *why* they had accepted his claims and theology as true, you might get the following responses: "He has confirmation from the spirit world," "Science proves that his theology is true," and "He has the true understanding of the Bible."

The importance of this approach is that if someone or some religious movement calls on us to give our total allegiance to them, then it should have the evidence to back up all claims made and demonstrate its truthfulness in an objective fashion. It should not have to rely on "indoctrination" and "behavior modification" as is implemented in the Unification centers. If it cannot demonstrate its truthfulness objectively, then we would be foolish to give our lives over to such a person or group. We would be following that which is false in a blind faith.

From the above responses, some claims regarding Rev. Moon and also some evidence for his theology has been gathered and categorized. These are the ones we want to examine in this section. Bear in mind that these are claims and evidence presented by the Unification Church. If Unification theology is supported by these, then it should be seriously considered and accepted as true. If it is not supported, then it should be rejected.

The place to begin is with the *Divine Principle*'s claim that Rev. Moon is a messenger of God. This is a claim that he and his followers continually assert. This can be tested as there are several criteria set forth which would determine whether or not he is a messenger of God. After all, if Rev. Moon is the fulfillment of the Judeo-Christian religion as claimed,[2] bringing us the "completed testament" regarding that which is presented in the Old and New Testament,[3] then he must meet the qualifications of such a messenger in that religion or historic faith of which he claims to be an extension. In the list of qualifications for the Lord of the

Second Advent, the Unification Church itself states that this must be so. In the *Divine Principle Study Guide* the Lord of the Second Advent must come "on behalf of God," the center of which "has been placed in Judeo Christianity. Therefore the work of the Lord must be based on this [Judeo Christianity]. . . ."[4] The context is explicit. If anyone does not meet the requirements of this basis as set forth in the Bible (that is the basis of Judeo Christianity), then that person could not be the Lord of the Second Advent.[5] If this is true of the Lord of the Second Advent, then it must also be true of Rev. Moon. With this in mind, let us look at these requirements as set forth in the Judeo-Christian Scriptures, the Bible.

First of all, a messenger of God must be in agreement with the previous divine revelation (the Old and New Testament) regarding the God he presents. The Bible specifically warns us in Deuteronomy 13:1-5 to watch out for self-proclaimed messengers of God because there are those who would lead us to follow and worship other gods than the one true biblical God. Never assume that such a person will necessarily tell you that this is what he intends, for an entirely different religion may be constructed around orthodox terminology. Unification theology does exactly this, as we have already seen.

Does Rev. Moon and the Unification Church proclaim the same God as the One portrayed in biblical Christianity? As we have already seen, the doctrine of God expounded by Rev. Moon is vastly different from that of biblical theology. The doctrine of creation accentuates the total difference, for in the Bible God brings the creation into existence out of nothing, while in Unification theology the creation flows or projects itself out of God's being or essence, so that it is part of God. Thus

Rev. Moon's doctrine of God totally contradicts the Bible.

The Unification Church might attempt to avoid this conclusion by claiming that the doctrines of God and creation presented in the previous section and used in this comparison are not those of the historic Christian Church. Such charges are groundless. They might also point to the diversity of Christendom through the ages with its interpretations and doctrines and claim that it would be impossible to come up with only one orthodox position.

It is true that Christianity has had its divisions along cultural lines and even over doctrinal points. No one would deny this. However, these divisions have never precluded the broad doctrinal agreement of what the late C. S. Lewis called *Mere Christianity*. Here we find tremendous historic agreement.

The Christian Church of all ages has set forth the same basic doctrines which include the doctrines of God and creation used in the previous section and in the above comparison. These very doctrines, held by all orthodox believers, are expressed in the ecumenical creeds throughout church history. As noted Church historian Philip Schaff writes: "Almost all the creeds of the first centuries, especially the Apostles' and the Nicene, begin with the confession of faith in God the Father Almighty, Maker of heaven and earth, of the visible and the invisible."[6] Of course one might ask, as does the Unification Church, what the historic definition of "Maker of heaven and earth" is and how the early church interpreted it and understood it. Schaff answers this in stating that "God made the world, including matter, not, of course out of any material, but out of nothing. . . ."[7]

The church fathers have also testified to this

throughout the centuries.[8] Their understanding was similar to that of Augustine who wrote: "For Thou didst create heaven and earth, not of Thyself, for then they would be equal to Thine only-begotten, and thereby even to Thee. . . . Therefore, out of nothing didst Thou create heaven and earth."[9] It is true that at least one church father, Origen, held a peculiar view of creation, maintaining that it was eternal,[10] and that a few of the church fathers expressed the doctrine of creation by using Platonic forms. But not one church father held to the doctrine that God created the world out of himself, as the Unification Church believes.

The historic Christian Church would unitedly voice its rejection of Rev. Moon as a messenger of God simply on the basis that the God he presents is not the God of the Bible as historically defined and understood. Therefore Rev. Moon could not be of that tradition.

Secondly, the prophecies of a messenger of God must always come to pass and be true. This test is set forth in Deuteronomy 18:22 where God says, "If a prophet speaks in the name of the Lord and the word does not happen nor come about, that is the word which the Lord has not spoken." In Isaiah 44:24–28 we see why this test will work. God promises that He will make fools of false messengers, but that He will uphold the predictions of His true messengers. One false prediction will prove that the message is not from God.

Though prophecies and predictions have not specifically been one of Rev. Moon's methods of presentation, nonetheless some of his statements could be understood as such, especially since they are revelations from God.

John Lofland, in his book *Doomsday Cult*, sets forth the claim of Rev. Moon that the Lord of the Second Advent would be revealed in 1967. This was not fulfilled and the new date chosen was 1980–81. Of course the Unification Church can work around this since they believe that in anything God's part is 95% and man's, 5%. It is man's part—that 5%—that makes the difference.

Many believed that the great "prophetic test" for Rev. Moon would come in 1980–81 (1960 plus 21 years for Jacob's age) at which time he had prophesied that the Lord of the Second Advent would be revealed and the kingdom of heaven would be inaugurated.

As far as we are concerned, this prophecy failed. Furthermore, it is falsified when examined in the light of historic Christianity. In order to make that prediction, Rev. Moon had to reject other statements and teaching in the Bible—doctrines given by God. For example, to have another Messiah necessitates the failure of the first Messiah—Jesus. It also requires the rejection of the return of Jesus. There are many other doctrines which could be brought in here to illustrate the point that Rev. Moon's prophecy is contrary to the Bible and thus could not follow from that historic basis. Any messenger of God prophesying such a contradiction would automatically have been rejected.

Thirdly, a messenger of the true God must be in agreement with the previous divine revelation (the Old and New Testament) regarding the person and work of Jesus Christ. This test is clearly set forth in 1 John 4:2, 3. Though the context is dealing with the Gnostic rejection of Jesus' coming in the flesh, the text is doctrinal in nature and centers around Jesus Christ. A wrong doctrine of Jesus, according to John, means a false messenger—one who is not of God. The New Testament stresses the fact that a true messenger of God will glorify Jesus as Deity, Redeemer, and Coming King.

How does Rev. Moon view Jesus? Is it really biblical? As we have seen in the previous section, Rev. Moon totally rejects a biblical Christology. In fact, Rev. Moon is in total disagreement with the major doctrines regarding the person and work of Jesus Christ.

The Unification Church might object to this conclusion by again stating that the doctrines presented and used in the comparison are not the doctrines of historic Christianity. Let's consider the crucial question of Jesus' deity. All the church fathers believed this doctrine[11] and its truth is expressed in the various ecumenical creeds.[12] As Philip Schaff notes: "This doctrine [Jesus as the God-man and Redeemer of the world] was the kernel of all baptismal creeds, and was stamped upon the life, constitution and worship of the early church."[13] Henry Parry Liddon says, "If there be one doctrine of our faith which the martyrs especially confessed at death, it is the doctrine of our Lord's Deity."[14] In like manner the victory of Jesus on the Cross, His bodily resurrection from the dead, and His coming again to judge the living and the dead are essential to the life and teachings of the early church. They are taught by the church fathers, expressed in the creeds, and have been central to the doctrinal beliefs of Christianity through the ages.

The historic Christian Church would unitedly voice its rejection of Rev. Moon as a messenger of God on the basis of his rejection of the person and work of Jesus Christ as set forth in the Bible.

So far we have examined only one of Rev. Moon's claims—that he is a messenger of God. The criteria used to evaluate this claim were three major areas presented in the Bible for such a test. There are other areas such as his teaching of "heavenly deception," which breaks the ninth commandment: "Thou shalt not bear false witness." A true messenger of God would teach the Ten Commandments, not break them and teach others to do likewise. Since Rev. Moon failed in all three areas when tested, his claim to be a messenger of God in the historic tradition of Judeo-Christianity cannot be substantiated. The evidence does not validate his claim; rather, it declares it to be false.

Another claim of Rev. Moon and the Unification Church to consider is his confirmation from the spirit world. Rev. Moon is, in fact, a practicing spiritist. He claims that through spiritism a person will know if he is the Lord of the Second Advent.[15] According to the Unification Church, spiritism is also the way any person can know that Rev. Moon is true. They claim the spirits will document their leader. "Those people who have sufficient communication with the spiritual world can receive direct confirmation concerning him. Such a person is Arthur Ford, a well-known Philadelphia sensitive."[16] What they are saying is that if you visit your friendly spiritist, he will bear witness to Rev. Moon. Interestingly, several spiritists have already rejected Moon!

This spiritism may be attractive to some, but there are several problems which need to be considered. First of all, the Bible expressly forbids indulging in such spiritistic practices (see Lev. 19:31; 20:6, 7; Deut. 18:11 and Isa. 8:19, 20). Certainly no man of God would involve himself in these practices.

Secondly, the Bible presents an alternative understanding of spiritism. It is not the surviving personalities of dead people which are contacted in séances, but demons (created spirit beings which do evil and follow Satan) which impersonate the dead. If Satan can transform himself into an angel of light, he can certainly disguise himself as a dead saint (see 2 Cor. 11:14). Spiritism might also help to explain Rev. Moon's rejection of biblical theology.

Dr. Walter R. Martin has written the following critique of spiritism:

> Spiritism as a cult has been from its beginning in opposition to the Judaeo-Christian religions. In order for one to embrace its teachings, every major doctrine of the Christian faith must be rejected, including the inspiration and final authority of the Bible, the doctrines of the Trinity, the Deity of Christ, the Virgin Birth, Vicarious Atonement, and Bodily Resurrection of our Lord from the grave. The Biblical doctrine of salvation by grace alone, apart from the works of the Law, is anathema to spiritist theology which relies on progressive evolution or growth in the "spirit world," to attain final perfection.[17]

Some similarities between Moon's theology and the above are obvious.

Thirdly, as William Peterson has observed, "Despite the fact that Moon claims to have talked with 'all the leaders in the Bible,' he still has a habit of contradicting them over and over again."[18] Of course the biblical interpretation of spiritism would explain why this is so. It was not the biblical leaders that he communicated with.

Fourthly, some of Rev. Moon's revelations contradict historical facts. For example, from the spirit world Rev. Moon concludes that Jesus did not rise bodily from the dead, but rather as a spirit man. Yet historic documents of that time period (the Gospels) and eyewitness accounts of people who lived then and saw Jesus in His resurrection body record and report the fact that Jesus rose bodily from the dead.[19] To deny this is to deny history itself, and yet this is exactly what Rev. Moon is asking us to do on the basis of his subjective spiritistic revelation. Philip Schaff states the problem this way: "Before one can reason the [bodily] resurrection of Christ

[Jesus] out of history, we must reason the apostles and Christianity itself out of history."[20] The fact that history declares some of the information Rev. Moon has received from his revelations as false should tell us that his revelations are not trustworthy. That these revelations contradict previous statements made by the same persons reinforces its untrustworthiness and make us wonder who or what it is he is contacting. The biblical interpretation of spiritism as demonism and not surviving personalities clearly expresses what Rev. Moon is involved in, explaining such elements as his non-biblical theology, false revelations, etc. Finally, this is all condemned in the Bible which tells us that such spiritistic involvement is totally untrustworthy.

The last claim we need to consider is that of science. That science supports their beliefs is basic to their approach to theology as set forth in their literature and lectures. Even out on the street corners when you hear a member giving a short lecture, the starting point is usually the same—scientific methodology. This procedure is clearly set forth in the *Divine Principle Study Guide*: "Scientists first advance a hypothesis, and then they develop theories to explain the phenomena which they are studying. When they find that these theories explain the phenomena accurately, their hypothesis is defined as a theorum. We will apply the same method to prove the existence of God."[21]

In actuality though, the Unification Church goes far beyond even modern physics in its explanation of the creation. Whereas science today would express what is here in terms of energy and matter, Rev. Moon teaches that matter is varying forms of energy (as modern physics states) which is one of the forms of God (here physics departs)—i.e., in God's essence this energy exists, and matter is varying forms of that energy. Biblical theology would differ with Rev. Moon in that it teaches that God made the creation (energy and matter) out of nothing and not out of himself.

The Unification Church has attempted to demonstrate its "scientific methods" in several other ways, the most notable being the International Conference of the Unity of the Sciences which it sponsors. Some time ago, the fourth one was held at the Waldorf Astoria in New York City. There were 300 scientists and engineers, including 17 Nobel Prize winners, invited. The stated purpose of the conference was to make some headway "towards the unification of science and religion." Others said it was a publicity move to gain worldwide attention and to give the appearance of scientific interests and teachings.

Unification Church spokesmen cite the importance of this conference, yet it should be noted that two of the five co-chairmen, sociologist Amitai Etzioni and economist Kenneth Boulding, resigned prior to the conference.[22] One of those who did attend the conference wrote a report of that conference which was published in the *New Engineer*. He stated that "most of the conferees remained distant from Moon's disciples and maintained no connection with his philosophy."[23]

To summarize, then, this section on the claims of Rev. Moon and the Unification Church, we have examined three areas: Christianity, spiritism, and science. Not one claim has been substantiated by the evidence, and beyond this there is additional evidence which contradicts the claims and theology of Rev. Moon. To test it further in other areas, especially in the realm of history (checking Rev. Moon's theological statements with that of biblical history), would only bring forth more evidence to the contrary. Thus the claims fail in their bid for credibility, leaving any seeker desperate for meaning and truth with no real basis for why one should give his life to Rev. Moon and the Unification Church. It also leaves us with the alternative explanations presented initially. Perhaps Moon is deluded, or a fraud, or demonically deceived. Whichever the case, he is not a messenger of God.

Because it has rejected the completed work of Jesus Christ and has replaced Him with the Lord of the Second Advent (a false Messiah), the Unification Church bypasses offering Jesus Christ as a live option for your life. The Bible records the history of this One as the God-man who demonstrated His deity in His message, by His works and miracles, and by His resurrection from the dead. He recognized the true condition of man as a sinner, estranged from God. This Jesus overcame the world, sin, and death, thus concreting man's hope in eternal life—not through visions and spiritistic revelations, but by sacrificing His life on Calvary's cross for our sins and by rising bodily from the dead. One day He is coming to set up His kingdom. This very Jesus wants you to give your life to Him and let Him be your Lord and Savior—a faith determined on the combined basis of objective evidence and subjective commitment. Jesus Christ is man's only true faith and hope, and to reject Him as a result of someone's warping the content and message of the Bible is assuredly tragic blindness.

NOTES

Notes to Chapter 1

1. *DPA*, p. vii.
2. *Sun Myung Moon*, p. 6; cf. *Master Speaks*, March and April, 1965, MS-3, pp. 4ff.
3. *DP*, p. 16.
4. *Time*, October 15, 1973, p. 129.
5. As quoted in William J. Peterson, *Those Curious New Cults*, New Canaan, Conn.: Keats Publishing Co., 1976, p. 250; cf. *Time*, June 14, 1976, p. 150 and Arao Arai, *The Madness of Japan*, Tokyo: Seison, 1975.
6. *Christian Century*, June 25, 1975, p. 647.
7. *DP*, p. 16.
8. E.g., UTCT, p. 234. Dr. Kim does not seem to find *many* parallels between the two Babylonian Captivities as the *Divine Principle* states.
9. *The Way of the World*, January 1975, p. 2.
10. *Minneapolis Star and Tribune*, Friday, Feb. 17, 1984.
11. John Cotter, "How Moon Wins Hearts and Minds," *New York Daily News*, Tuesday, December 2, 1975, p. 38.
12. *Time*, August 16, 1976, pp. 31ff.
13. *Time*, June 14, 1976, p. 50.
14. See Ted Patrick, *Let My Children Go*, New York: Dutton, 1976, for accounts of deprogramming and their explanations.

Notes to Chapter 2

1. *UTCT*, p. 2.
2. E.g., *DP, DPA, DPSG, PC*.

3. *UTCT*, p. 2.
4. *DPSG*, p. 14.
5. *DPA*, p. 5; cf. *DPSG*, p. 8.
6. *UTCT*, p. 7.
7. E.g., *DPA*, pp. 3, 5; cf. *DPSG*, pp. 13ff. and *DP*, p. 25.
8. *DPSG*, p. 16; cf. *DP*, pp. 26–7. Note the differences which are pointed out between Unification theology and Taoist philosophy. While some elements, such as the Sung-Sang and Hyung-Sang and that which is involved in the process to produce "all the creation," are different, *the overall system and framework is identical*. In both cases, everything projects out from God, dualism forms the basis for all manifestations, and everything finds its explanation and existence in God's essence.
9. E.g., *DPSG*, pp. 30ff.
10. *DPSG*, p. 8.
11. *PC*, p. 13; cf. *DPSG*, p. 16 and *DP*, p. 25.
12. *DPA*, p. 2; cf. *DPSG*, p. 15; *DP*, p. 40 and *UTCT*, p. 7.
13. *PC*, p. 22; cf. *DPSG*, p. 24.
14. *UTCT*, p. 7.
15. *DPA*, pp. 24–5.
16. *DPSG*, pp. 46ff.
17. *DP*, pp. 60ff.
18. *DPSG*, pp. 62ff.
19. *DPA*, pp. 3, 11; cf. *DPSG*, p. 64.
20. *DPSG*, p. 36.
21. *PC*, p. 52.
22. *DPSG*, p. 38; cf. *DP*, p. 53.
23. *DPA*, p. 41; cf. *DPSG*, p. 26 and *DP*, p. 57.
24. *DPA*, p. 77; cf. *DPSG*, p. 26.
25. *DPA*, p. 41.
26. *DPA*, p. 38; cf. *DPSG*, pp. 81–3 and *DP*, pp. 72–3.
27. *DPSG*, pp. 83–4; cf. *DP*, p. 72–3.
28. *DPA*, pp. 64–5; cf. *DPSG*, p. 83.
29. *DPA*, p. 77.
30. *DPSG*, p. 129.
31. *DPSG*, p. 129; cf. *DP*, p. 139.
32. *DPA*, p. 75; cf. *DPSG*, p. 192 and *DP*, pp. 211ff.
33. *DP*, p. 212; cf. *DPSG*, pp. 129, 194.
34. *DPA*, pp. 64–5; cf. *DP*, pp. 140–1.
35. *DP*, pp. 209–13.
36. *DPA*, pp. 64–5.

37. *DP*, p. 143; cf. *DPSG*, p. 133.
38. Rev. Sun Myung Moon, *Christianity in Crisis*; cf. *DPSG*, pp. 149–54 and *DP*, pp. 157ff.
39. *DPSG*, p. 138.
40. *DP*, p. 212.
41. *DPSG*, pp. 139, 165; cf. *DP*, pp. 147ff.
42. *DPSG*, p. 197.
43. *DPA*, p. 71.
44. *DP*, p. 510.
45. *DP*, pp. 500, 510.
46. *DP*, p. 520.
47. *DP*, p. 177.
48. *DP*, p. 179; cf. *DPA*, pp. iv, vii.
49. *DPA*, p. 196.
50. *Ibid.*
51. *DP*, pp. 184ff.; cf. *DPSG*, p. 172.
52. *DPSG*, pp. 169ff.; cf. *DPA*, pp. 24–5 and *DP*, pp. 182ff.
53. *DPSG*, pp. 174ff.; cf. *DP*, pp. 157ff.
54. *DPA*, p. 50.
55. *DPSG*, pp. 179ff.; cf. *DPA*, p. 194 and *DP*, pp. 188ff.
56. *DP*, p. 194.
57. *DP*, p. 452.
58. Colossians 2:9.
59. *DP*, pp. 210–11.
60. Acts 2:23.
61. *DP*, p. 143.
62. Luke 24:39.
63. *DP*, p. 212.
64. Acts 1:11.
65. *DP*, p. 513.
66. *DP*, p. 534.
67. Mortimer J. Adler, *How to Read a Book*, New York: Simon & Schuster, 1940, sets forth some basic principles for use with any literature. For a comprehensive basis regarding the principles used in interpreting the Bible, see William C. Lincoln, *Personal Bible Study*, Minneapolis, Minnesota: Bethany House, 1975.
68. As quoted in *Eternity*, April 1976, p. 27.
69. *DPA*, p. 194.
70. John 14:6.
71. Acts 4:12.
72. As quoted in *Time*, September 30, 1974, p. 68.

73. *Newsweek*, October 15, 1973, p. 54.
74. *The Boston Phoenix*, July 23, 1974, p. 10.
75. John 18:38.
76. Matthew 7:20.
77. Matthew 7:21–2.
78. Matthew 7:23.

Notes to Chapter 3

1. *DP*, p. 16.
2. E.g., *DP*, pp. 232–8; cf. *DPA*, p. vii and *DPSG*, pp. 163–73.
3. E.g., *DP*, p. 137; cf. *DPSG*, pp. 5–6.
4. *DPSG*, p. 167.
5. *Ibid.*
6. Philip Schaff, *History of the Christian Church*, Vol. II, p. 536.
7. *Ibid.*, p. 540.
8. E.g., Tatian, *Address to the Greeks*, 5; Irenaeus, *Adversus Haereses*, 2.10; Clement of Alexandria, *Stromata*, 5:14; and John Scotus Erigena, *Of the Divineness of Nature*, 3.5, 14.
9. Augustine, *Confessions*, 13.7.
10. Origen, *De principiis*, 1.3.10.
11. E.g., Ignatius, *Ephesus*, 7.2; 15:3; 18:2; *Romans*, 3.3; 6.3; Athenagorus, *Plea for the Christians*, 10; Tertullian, *Against Praxeas*, 2; and Origen, *Contra Celsus*, 1. VIII, 67.
12. E.g., the Nicaeno-Constantinopolitan Creeds and Athanasian Creed.
13. Schaff, *op. cit.*, p. 545.
14. Henry Parry Liddon, *The Divinity of Our Lord and Saviour Jesus Christ*, p. 406.
15. *DP*, 529ff.
16. *Sun Myung Moon*, p. 6.
17. Walter R. Martin, *Kingdom of the Cults*, Minneapolis: Bethany House, 1969, p. 212.
18. William Peterson, *op. cit.*, p., 259.
19. For a study of the historical method applied to Christianity, see John Warwick Montgomery, *History and Christianity*, Downer's Grove, Ill.; InterVarsity Press, 1969. This is also published in his *Where Is History Going?*, Minneapolis: Bethany House, 1969, chapters 2 and 3.

20. Schaff, *op. cit.*, Vol. I, p. 183.
21. *DPSG*, p. 1.
22. *Christian Century*, September 24, 1975, p. 812.
23. Cy Adler, "A Moon Shines on Science," *New Engineer*, Vol. V, No. 3, March 1976, pp. 39–41.

Other books in this series:

Christian Science
Herbert W. Armstrong
Horoscopes and the Christian
Jehovah's Witnesses
Mormonism
Reincarnation and Christianity
Hypnosis and the Christian